Vanita's Dedication

This book is dedicated to:
Lily
and all my other grandchildren

Kristin's Dedication

Dedicated to the sweetest girls in the world:
Sage, Vi-yen, and Maddie

Acknowledgements

Many thanks to:

Kristin Blackwood

Mike Blanc

Kurt Landefeld

Paul Royer

Carolyn Brodie

Sheila Tarr

Jennie Levy Smith

Ivy in Bloom
VanitaBooks, LLC
All rights reserved.
© 2009 VanitaBooks, LLC

Text by Vanita Oelschlager.
Illustrations by Kristin Blackwood.
Design by Mike Blanc.

Printed in China.
ISBN 978-0-9800162-7-7

www.VanitaBooks.com

Ivy in Bloom

The POETRY of SPRING

from GREAT POETS *and* WRITERS *of the* PAST

By VANITA OELSCHLAGER

ILLUSTRATED *by* KRISTIN BLACKWOOD

VanitaBooks, LLC

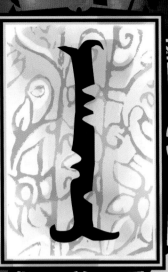 **I**'m Ivy Van Allsberg.

I'm waiting for spring.

I stare out the window

Looking for birds

Or flowers

Or even warm showers.

But I don't see any such thing.

The world's a smudge
Of brown and gray.
The buds won't budge
The sun stays away.

When, oh when,
Will spring be here?
When will outside be
Yellow and blue,
Green and red
And bright orange too?

Winter winds are piercing chill.

It was one of those March days

when the sun shines hot and the wind blows cold.

Clouds hang heavy and gray.

The fountain holds up
its chandeliers of frost.

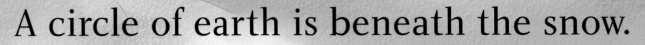

A circle of earth is beneath the snow.

Spring, when the world is mud-luscious.

Spring, when the world is puddle-wonderful.

April prepares her
green traffic light
And the world thinks,
"GO!"

Give me sunbeams dazzling.

March, how out of breath you are!

April comes strewing flowers.

These flowery waters and these watery flowers
from snow that melted only yesterday.

Spring arose from its wintry rest.

Heart dances with daffodils.

She wore her yellow sun-bonnet
She wore her greenest gown.

God's in His heaven, all's right with the world!

Ivy in Bloom

The POETRY of SPRING

from GREAT POETS and WRITERS of the PAST

BIBLIOGRAPHY

Lines in green were used for the illustrations.

When, oh when,
Will spring be here?
When will outside be
Yellow and blue,
Green and red
And bright orange too?

Vanita Oelschlager wrote:

I'm Ivy Van Allsberg.
I'm waiting for spring.
I stare out the window
Looking for birds
Or flowers
Or even warm showers.
But I don't see any such thing.

Henry Wadsworth Longfellow wrote:

When winter winds are piercing chill,
And through the hawthorne blows the gale,
With solemn feet I tread the hill,
That overbrows the lonely vale.

O'er the bare upland, and away
Through the long reach of desert woods,
The embracing sunbeams chastely play,
And gladden those deep solitudes.

Henry Wadwsorth Longfellow lived from 1807-1883.
He was an American educator and lyric poet.
This comes from the poem **Woods in Winter**.

The world's a smudge
Of brown and gray.
The buds won't budge
The sun stays away.

Charles Dickens wrote:

It was one of those March days
When the sun shines hot
And the wind blows cold:
When it is summer in the light,
And winter in the shade.

Charles Dickens lived from 1812-1870. He was an English novelist generally considered the greatest of the Victorian era. This comes from his novel **Great Expectations**.

William Cullen Bryant wrote:

Stand here by my side and turn, I pray.
On the lake below thy gentle eyes;
The clouds hang over it, heavy and gray
And dark and silent the water lies;
And out of that frozen mist the snow
In wavering flakes begins to flow;
Flake after flake
They sink in the dark and silent lake.

William Cullen Bryant lived from 1794-1878. He was an American Romantic Poet, journalist and long-time editor of The New York Post. This comes from his poem **The Snow Shower**.

John Greenleaf Whittier wrote:

A sound as if from bells of silver,
Or elfin cymbals smitten clear,
Through the frost-pictured panes I hear.

A brightness which outshines the morning.
A splendor brooking no delay,
Beckons and tempts my feet away.

I leave the trodden village highway
For virgin snow-paths glimmering through
A jeweled elm-tree avenue;

Where, keen against the walls of sapphire,
The gleaming tree-bolls, ice-embossed,
Hold up their chandeliers of frost.

John Greenleaf Whittier lived from 1807-1892. He was an influential American Quaker poet. This comes from his poem **The Pageant**.

William Cullen Bryant also wrote:

And 'neath the hemlock, whose
    Thick branches bent
Beneath its bright cold burden, and
    Kept dry
A circle, on the earth, of withered
    Leaves,
The Partridge found a shelter.
    Through the snow
The rabbit spring away. The
    Lighter track
Of fox, and the raccoon's broad
    Path, were there,
Crossing each other. From his
    Hollow tree
The squirrel was abroad, gathering
    The nuts
Just fallen, that asked the winter
    Cold and sway
Of winter blast to shake them from their hold.

William Cullen Bryant is previously listed.
This comes from his poem **A Winter Piece**.

e.e. cummings wrote:

Spring
when the world is mud-luscious.
Spring
when the world is puddle-wonderful.

e.e. cummings lived from 1894-1962. He was an
American poet, painter, essayist, author and playwright.
This comes from **In Just**, *published in 1920.*

Christopher Morley wrote:

April prepares her green traffic light
And the world thinks Go.

Christopher Morley lived from 1890-1957. He was an
American poet, novelist, journalist, and playwright.
This comes from **John Mistletoe**, *written in 1931.*

Edna St. Vincent Millay wrote:

To what purpose, April do you return again
Beauty is not enough.
You can no longer quiet me with the redness
Of little leaves opening stickily…
April,
Comes like an idiot, babbling, and strewing
flowers.

Edna St. Vincent Millay lived from 1892-1950. She was the first woman to receive the Pulitzer Prize for poetry. She was an American Lyrical poet. This comes from her poem **Spring,** *from her book* **Second April**.

Robert Frost wrote:

The trees that have in their pent-up buds
To darken nature and be summer woods
Let them think twice before they use their powers
To blot out and drink up and sweep away
These flowery waters and these watery flowers
From snow that melted only yesterday.

Robert Frost lived from 1874-1963. He was an American poet. This poem named **Spring Pools,** *comes from his first volume,* **West-Running Brook**.

Walt Whitman wrote:

Give me the splendid silent sun
With all his beams full-dazzling.

Walt Whitman lived from 1819-1892. He was an American poet, essayist, journalist, and humanist. This comes from **Leaves of Grass**.

Emily Dickinson wrote:

Dear March, come in!
How glad I am!
I hoped for you before.
Put down your hat -
You must have walked -
How out of breath you are!
Dear March, how are you?
And the rest?
Did you leave Nature well?
Oh, March, come right upstairs with me,
I have so much to tell!

Emily Dickinson lived from 1830-1886. She was an American poet. This poem comes from **Dear March Come In**.

Percy Bysshe Shelley wrote:

And Spring arose on the garden fair,
Like the Spirit of Love felt everywhere;
And each flower and herb on Earth's dark breast
Rose from the dreams of its wintry rest.

Percy Bysshe Shelley lived from 1792-1822. He was a major English Romantic poet. This comes from **The Sensitive Plant***.*

Thomas Nashe wrote:

Spring, the sweet spring, is the year's
    pleasant king;
Then blooms each thing, then maids dance in
    a ring,
Cold doth not sting, the pretty birds do sing.
Cuckoo, jug, jug, pu-we, to- witte, woo!

Thomas Nashe lived from 1567-1601. He was an English poet. This comes from **Summer's Last Will and Testament***.*

William Wordsworth wrote:

I wander lonely as a cloud,
That floats on high o'er vales and hills,
When all at once I saw a crowd,
A host of golden daffodils;
Beside the lake, beneath the trees,
Fluttering and dancing in the breeze…
And then my heart with pleasure fills
And dances with the daffodils.

William Wordsworth lived from 1770-1850. He was an English Romantic poet. This comes from **I Wander Lonely as a Cloud***. Some people call this poem* **Daffodils***.*

A.A. Milne wrote:

She wore her yellow sun-bonnet
She wore her greenest gown;
She turned to the south wind
And curtsied up and down
She turned to the sunlight
And shook her yellow head,
And whispered to her neighbor:
"Winter is dead."

A.A. Milne lived from 1882-1956. He was an English playwright and the author of **Winnie the Pooh***. This poem named* **Daffodowndilly***, comes from his collection called* **When We Were Young***, and was written in 1924.*

Robert Browning wrote:

The year's at the spring
And day's at the morn;
Morning's at seven;
The hill-side's dew-pearled;
The lark's on the wing;
The snail's on the thorn;
God's in His heaven –
All's right with the world!

Robert Browning lived from 1812-1889. He was an English poet and playwright. This poem comes from **The Year's at the Spring***.*

Vanita Oelschlager

Vanita Oelschlager is a wife, mother, grandmother, former teacher, caregiver, author and poet. She was named "Writer in Residence" for the Literacy Program at The University of Akron in 2007. She is a graduate of Mount Union College, Alliance, Ohio, where she is currently a member of the Board of Trustees.

Kristin Blackwood

Kristin Blackwood is an experienced illustrator whose other books include: *My Grampy Can't Walk, Let Me Bee, What Pet Will I Get?, Made in China,* and *Big Blue.* She has a degree from Kent State University in Art History. In addition to teaching and her design work, Kristin enjoys being a mother to her two daughters.

About the Art

Kristin's illustration is a blending of techniques, beginning with traditional block prints, cut in linoleum, and printed in black on white stock. The images were converted to digital format through flatbed scanning. Watercolor layers were added using Corel® Painter™, and Adobe® Photoshop®, computer software for digital illustration. The result, presented here, is a playful visual note for *Ivy in Bloom*.

Profits

All net profits from this book will be donated to charitable organizations, with a gentle preference towards serving people with my husband's disease – multiple sclerosis.

Vanita

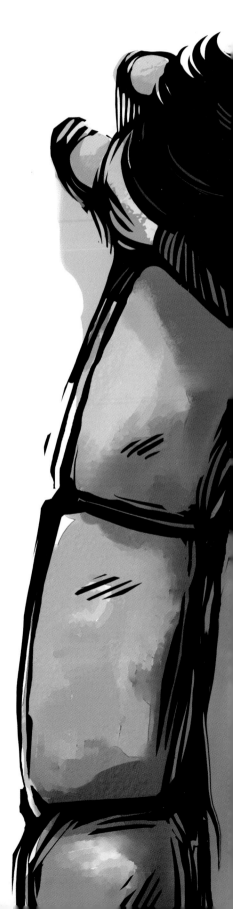